# Scottish Steam Days Remembered

Strathwood

# Scottish Steam Days Remembered

Front Cover: Just a short while away from being withdrawn and thankfully heading for preservation in December 1966, we see that stalwart for Scottish steam 60532 Blue Peter on her then home shed of Aberdeen Ferryhill on 17 June 1966. *Rail Photoprints*

## Strathwood

# Scottish Steam Days Remembered

A selection of some of the essential books and magazines from the era along with a few other reminders of the locomotives.

First published 2017
ISBN 1-905276-73-7
ISBN 978-1-905276-73-8

Copyright Strathwood Publishing 2017
Published by Strathwood Publishing, 9 Boswell Crescent, Inverness, IV2 3ET
Telephone 01463 234004
Printed by Akcent Media

# Contents

**Page**

# Preface

This volume has been in my mind for some time in order to share some of my favourite colour shots from Scotland's British Railways steam days for some time. In compiling this collection a number of views have had to be omitted for fear of accusations of bias towards certain classes or locations. Therefore I am sure if this volume is successful we will come back and revisit the region once more for another selection.

This has also given me the chance to provide a platform to share some reminiscences from a long term friend Peter Coton whose acquaintance I had the pleasure of making almost thirty years ago in Perth in Western Australia. Through the wonders of email we remain in touch to this day within a close group of friends across the globe who share a passion for British Railways steam.

We will all have our favourites from the past, I hope you will enjoy this compilation and we must also thank the foresight of the photographers and the kindness of those who have allowed their work to be seen and appreciated by a wider audience.

**Kevin Derrick**
**Inverness 2017**

Above: Unrebuilt Scot 46148 The Manchester Regiment is well assisted in the rear by a 2-6-4T on the heavy climb past Harthope with a Carlisle to Glasgow service, in July 1953. *Dave Cobbe Collection/Rail Photoprints*

# Introduction -

In many ways, Scotland should have become a magnet for me some time before the penny finally dropped. After all, there were so many attractions and not the very least were the multiple locations where ex LMS Pacifics rubbed noses with their East Coast counterparts, with representatives of all the BR Standard Pacifics adding further to the mix.

A holiday in the Lake District during 1954 should have been the prompt. We had a St. Swithins summer that year and the chances of keeping a 12 year-old amused with the views of another soggy lake seen from the restricted back seat of an Alvis Grey Lady were close to absolute zero. So as often as not I was down at Keswick station, where the former Cockermouth. Keswick & Penrith had a healthy service of Ivatt 2-6-0's on the passengers and the odd appearance of 'Cauliflowers' 58412 or 58427 on the occasional goods.

The crew of 60034 Lord Faringdon top up the tender for the 17.15 Aberdeen to Glasgow express during the Perth stop on 18 July 1966. *Bill Wright*

On each of the Wednesdays I was given enough to take me off to Carlisle, gateway to Scotland. Indeed Carlisle Kingmoor had a period in the '50's of being coded 68A, thus considered part of the Scottish Region. On Penrith station I made a schoolboy clanger and asked a fellow young spotter what a Stratford Britannia was doing on the LNW mainline. He looked suitably bemused until I showed him my note of 72001 amongst the Corkerhill Jubilees and Polmadie Scots and Duchesses. Realisation dawned - "that woz no Brit, it were a Clan". Oops, but I had never clapped eyes on one of those before.

On the middle Sunday my folks decided that a coach trip to Edinburgh would relieve the tedium of monsoon conditions and off we went. Coffee stop at Moffat, nowhere near the branch line terminus and then eventually into Auld Reekie. All the touristy things to fit into a few hours but I was going no further than Waverley station. Oh, and how pleased I was to do so, with no fewer than five A4 'cops' in twenty minutes.

It was a good few years later until I next went back, Summer 1963 in fact. A camping holiday with only passing railway interest, truly a wasted opportunity. It was '65 before we went again, but this time with the avowed intent of seeing what was left whilst it still drew breath. In Edinburgh, St. Margarets was still very much worth a visit, but it was already a shadow of what had gone before, even with the influx of survivors from Haymarket, now firmly the northern base of the all-conquering Deltics. Arrival there after the drive from the home counties was in time to see 60142 Kenilworth, then one of the Darlington stand-by Pacifics, come on shed after heading a troop train from Richmond, in Yorkshire and 60034 Lord Farringdon shunting an effulgent Prince Palatine, all bulled up for the following day's A3 farewell trip. Sadly 60052 expired at Carlisle with a hot box, being replaced by a grimy 60027 Merlin for the trip back over the soon to be doomed Waverley route.

The rest of that holiday involved a rather depressing shed-bash. Oh yes, plenty of underlining of obscure NB and Caley locos, but most of them seen rusting away at places like Polmont, Bo'ness, Grangemouth and

Bathgate. The latter was a temporary reprieve for some of Haymarket's finest and included Pearl Diver, Irish Elegance and Bachelor's Button. At this time of mass slaughter, nothing was immune and the venerable Caley tanks and NB 0-6-0s which had completed a worthy shift of sixty or more years were cheek by jowl with modern V1 and V3 tanks, post war Pacifics and Black 5s, together with WDs of both 2-8-0 and 2-10-0 variants.

But steam was by no means finished and the surviving A4s were dominating the three hour Glasgow - Aberdeen service. 60052 lingered on for a few more months, whilst the last A1s barely turned a wheel at Darlington, York and Tweedmouth. Polmadie had turned its nose up at the allocation of a few A2s with 60512 soon withdrawn and despatched, 60535 left to rust at the back of the shed and 60530 kicked back to Dundee where it lingered to become the penultimate survivor. How the shedmasters must have cursed the bean-counters who had prematurely robbed them of their Stanier Pacifics, leading to much unnecessary double heading over Shap and Beattock for the next three years.

But we could write volumes about the stupidity of the headlong dash to dieselisation, the appalling waste of life expectancy of 999 British Railway's standard locos and many other locos built post war and written off with years of useful life ahead.

Brightening up, although not on the weather front, a visit to a Thornton Junction shed shrouded in mist, in and out of which shuffled a variety locos. J36 antiques shared the spotlight with the powerful J38s, Thompson B1s and WDs. At least in this part of Fife the old order was fighting on, but the wonderful variety of a few years previously - D11, D30 and D34 4-4-0s had all gone to meet their maker, and many of the lovely lines around the Fife coast that they had served so well had not been saved by the ubiquitous DMUs .

Even as late as the mid sixties, there were not so many enthusiasts who drove cars. It was quite amazing how the presence of a car was almost as good as a shed permit. Somehow it appeared that anyone who drove their own car had to be 'legitimate', and entry was seldom refused. Initially I would drive into a shed yard and park up as far as possible from the entrance, necessitating a slow walk past everything that I wanted to see en route to asking permission. As this seemed pretty well infallible, I

Black 5, 44997 is being prepared for duty on shed at Perth.
*Strathwood Library Collection*

got bolder and would park close to the shedmaster's office and take it from there. Of course there were places where it simply didn't work, like Dundee Tay Bridge, located as it was between the lines to Tay Bridge and West stations, and with no direct road access. But Dundee never refused me access, and until very late in the piece had their three A2s - 60528/30/32 - parked outside waiting for photographers. One would usually take the afternoon fitted freight to Millerhill and all were known to stretch their legs once a week on a trip to Glasgow and give a BR Caprotti 5 a rest. Dundee also saw the last real concentration of V2s, arguably my favourite loco. Amongst the last seven to survive was the unique 'shovel-rim deflector' fitted 60813.

I had three "all-line" Railrovers in 1966, mainly to bash the Glasgow - Aberdeen line, All the nutters, amongst whom I proudly number myself, showed remarkable stamina at this time, mainly designed to rinse the absolute maximum value from our tickets. Of course, there were many who got superb value by simply not buying tickets at all, but I reckoned that with the freedom of mainland UK and the Clyde steamers, etc, £18.00 for a week was not too high a price to pay.

My routine involved staying up all night every other night, using either the 23.30 Glasgow - Aberdeen (which of course positioned you for the following morning's 07.10 out of the Granite City), or the "Northern Irishman", due off Ayr just before midnight for the run to Carlisle. Both were high prospects for a footplate run and I was successful on the 23.30 with Bittern out to Stirling and twice with Britannia's down to Dumfries. On the first occasion, I was negotiating the deal as the Black 5 pilot up from Stranraer was being detached and was invited up. No time to put my case in the front carriage, it came up with me. And I was immediately invited to get my jacket off and take the shovel. At 23 years of age, I was fit enough for the task but nevertheless was breathless by Mauchline, and very pleased to be relieved by a grinning fireman. A few nights later, with the same crew I was excused firing duties, but invited to operate the water scoop on New Cumnock troughs. Apparently the 1,300 gallons I collected was sufficient to avoid having to put the bag in at Dumfries.

I had another super footplate run with unnamed 70047 from Carlisle to Carstairs, one night with a heavy parcels train. As we passed Lockerbie, I asked the driver if he proposed to stop at Beattock, which earned me an old-fashioned look and the response "Och, dinna wanna banker". The Britannias were clearly masters of the job, but I did feel that they were hungry!

For Easter 1967 the BR Scottish Region ran an ambitious railtour which started in Edinburgh, traversed the Waverley route and then ran from Carlisle over Beattock to Perth and Aberdeen. I joined at Carlisle, having cadged a lift from a work colleague who was on a rugby tour to Halifax. The memory dims as to how I spent Good Friday evening getting to Carlisle, but I found myself on the Saturday morning watching as the tour arrived - eighteen full coaches with D368/D1973 at the front. These ran around and we set off for Perth with much speculation as to how 60009 was meant to cope with this load on the steam section to Aberdeen. The story goes that Mr Cameron, who now owned No.9,

Another of 63A Perth's large allocation of Black 5s, 44698 finds itself at Balornock in August 1965.
*Strathwood Library Collection*

once again to take over the final leg, back to Edinburgh via Gleneagles and Stirling - an unadvertised bonus! Even then, the organisers hadn't finished, as they had thoughtfully arranged for the "Aberdonian" overnight sleeper to King's Cross to be held for 15 minutes to enable the connection. I slept well that night and caught the "Excursion" out of Waterloo the following morning. Dribbling down to Woking, stopping at Wimbledon and Surbiton behind 34098 Templecombe, I shared the previous day's exploits with a largely unbelieving front compartment of those who had endured the electrification-riddled slacks of the LSWR main line.

Scotland seemed so far away for a lad living in Wadhurst in 1954, and indeed it was. For it was nine years later that I wasted a camping holiday in Scotland by almost totally ignoring the railways. Instead of concentrating on what was living, I went to the graveyards of Bo'ness, Bathgate, Polmont and Grangemouth and took only eighteen pictures, including 44754/65930, which appeared in the October 1991 "Glorious Years" feature of Steam World. It was also notable for being refused entry to Kingmoor at the end of the tour, but a chance meeting with the celebrated photographer Charles Newton on Citadel station proved fortuitous. He had a permit, and I had a car! So I duly presented myself for a second time at Kingmoor and this time gained entry, underlining Duchess of Norfolk in my notebook and clearing the class.

had been told it would need a BRCW Type 2 pilot and that in turn he had felt this would be a breach of faith for the punters, who had paid good money for a steam run. So when we rolled into Perth, Union of South Africa was coupled up with 63A's last Black 5, 44997. No one who was on that trip will ever forget it as the pair whisked this huge train (615 tons tare and probably 680 tons gross) up to Aberdeen in even time, achieving 80 mph after crossing the Tay and again at Farnell Road.

Everyone spent the next part of the tour comparing notes of the performance, as we wound our way north, via the sinuous Speyside line to Aviemore, now with two Sulzer Type 2s (D5127/D5070) at the front. At that stage, a third member of the class (D5122) was added for the trip south to Perth over Druimauchdar. Thus when we arrived at Perth, it was to find that the two steam locos had run back light and were on duty

I had a bout of temporary insanity in 1964 and went to Jersey on holiday, but was sufficiently recovered to head north again in 1965 as already mentioned a visit to St. Margarets shed saw 60034 pulling 60052 around ahead of the A3 farewell trip the following day. Sadly, the A3 expired at Carlisle and was replaced by a grubby 60027 for my only run over the Waverley Route. We established our campsite at Greenloaning and spent a week photographing and travelling on the Glasgow – Aberdeen line. During the course of that we witnessed the last few runs of 72006, and the final two Scots – 46115/40, but it was clear that the writing was truly on the wall. Polmadie had the hated A2s 60512/35, but both were withdrawn.

Back to Easter 1966 once more and the first of the three all-line Railrovers once more, I set out on Thursday 7 April, Jubilees 45562/5 were seen in the Leeds area on the way up and a distressed 70003 derailed at Hellifield. The following morning at Dundee, 60530/2 were busy doing nothing as usual, but (the infamous) 60919 was getting special attention, later to work the afternoon train from Perth to Buchanan St. and thereafter scheduled to take a railtour the following day. I mentioned this to the normal tribe on the 1.30 Aberdeen – Glasgow, which encouraged the majority to get off and wait for the V2. Not only was I relieved to find 60919 take up this duty, but also that I didn't go on the tour, which crossed the Forth bridge rather late the following day and behind Paxman engined D6123 as the V2 had failed. Incidentally, the Stephenson link Black 5 44767 was ex works from Cowlairs and on station pilot duty prior to returning to its Kingmoor home.

Scotland was "Steamless" on Sundays, so I returned overnight and did a "fill-in" turn to Southampton and a night in my own bed before heading north on Monday. Retracing my steps from Thursday (King's Cross – Leeds – Carnforth – Glasgow) and thence the 11.00 to Aberdeen. I slept on the early morning stopper to Perth, back to Aberdeen and then the 1.30 right through to Buchanan St. and the overnight train south. Wednesday was in Weymouth, but outside the remit of this tale !

Whitsun saw round 2. I started in Leeds with 45581 to Blackpool and back on the Holiday Monday and then after a lift from a pal south to Derby, the sleeper to Glasgow. The routine was to bash the A4's during daylight and then either take the Britannia on the Northern Irishman (23.55 off Ayr) to Carlisle or the A4 on the 23.00 to Aberdeen. Occasionally I would do neither and have a proper nights sleep, but not often as there was still much to enjoy!
For the August Bank Holiday the active A4's were down to just two

Right: Locally allocated to 62C, Thompson B1, 61101 is on an easy working with a mixed goods near Dunfermline on 1 June 1966.
*Strathwood Library Collection*

60019/24 and it was clear that they were on borrowed time. But I took a last glance and got a final All Line Railrover. In fact, I found as we travelled through Larbert in midweek that my ticket had been mistakenly issued for two weeks, amazingly as the expiry had to be changed from August (one week) to September. I wondered what to do with this "bonus" week and eventually decided against seeing it out in Scotland, not least as I had to be back at work from Monday to Friday in London! But for the first week in Scotland and the highlight was on the Friday. The 9.25 Crewe – Perth was extended FO to Aberdeen. A number of us had intended to catch this from Perth and then to enjoy Blue Peter's final southbound run.

As the time went by and the Crewe train failed to emerge, we were busy recalculating our options, concluding that we might have to get off at Stonehaven, or even cut our losses and travel to Dundee. Waiting to take over the train was 70014, disguised in a heavy coat of grime and looking far from fit for purpose. The driver was sitting on his grease-proof cap on the rail behind the tender and I volunteered to "negotiate" with him. It turned out that he had an urgent appointment that required him to get the Edinburgh train as well, so as long as the blessed train from the south arrived, we still had chances. Eventually it came in and

off we went. And my word, we flew, Coupar Angus involved a slow pass with shouted confirmation that no-one wanted to get off, ditto Forfar. I scrambled onto the footplate at Bridge of Dun and we took Kinnaber Junction with a healthy disregard of the speed restriction and by Stonehaven it was worth a punt to stay on board. We rolled in to Aberdeen with 5 minutes to spare and the driver several pounds better off for his efforts. Afterwards 60532 pottered down to Edinburgh, but it was an anti-climax compared with what had gone before.

It wasn't quite the end of my Scottish trips as I think back once again to Easter 1967 and the previously described run with 60009 and 44997 on one of the outstanding runs of the steam era. Leaving Perth, the pair were quickly into their stride with the first "80" achieved as we crossed the upper reaches of the Tay. The old rivalries continued to arise, with Stanier afficionados marvelling at their steed's puissance whilst Gresley followers talked in hushed terms about their man's engine's ability to pull the train whilst pushing the Black 5 – exhilarating stuff indeed!

My swansong on the Strathmore line was on my 24th birthday - a run from Glasgow Central to Aberdeen and back with the preserved A4 Sir Nigel Gresley. This came about as 1967 was one of the few years of that decade that I failed to get an FA Cup Final ticket, particularly disappointing as my team, Spurs, despatched Chelsea 2-1 that day. So it was then that my final trip to Scotland in "real" steam days came on 20 May 1967, but with the by then privately owned "4498 Sir Nigel Gresley". Matters were already changing, Buchanan St. had shut and our train left from Glasgow Central, so here we had a long trek around the south and east of the city before finding the old haunts at Cumbernauld. It wasn't a great re-acquaintance with the glory days of the Strathmore line, but we duly arrived in Aberdeen, and the return journey was via Montrose, Dundee, Dunfermline and the Forth Bridge before turning right for Glasgow.

Fifty years later, I have fond memories of the time spent in Scotland, mixed with the feeling that I should have done so much more. But the same is true of so many other areas of the land – Cornwall with the Counties and Granges, The Cambrian with the Manors and later BR 4MT's, the final days of the North East, etc. I am grateful for the opportunity to witness the Indian summer of the A4's and all the other stuff in Scotland that was going on at the time, even though the run-down state of a lot of the locos meant that a good run was hard to find.

Peter Coton
Essex 2017

Fowler 4MT, 42320 was still allocated to Barrow when this shot was taken in 1960 at Beattock, withdrawn in November 1962 it would work its last two years out of Carlisle Kingmoor. *Strathwood Library Collection*

Opposite: From the 65B St. Rollox allocation of Black 5s, 45125 barks away northwards from Beattock in 1960. *Strathwood Library Collection*

**Beattock Stopover**

A heavy northbound service behind 46203 Princess Margaret Rose, has stopped to take on the assistance of one of Beattock's many banking engines as both engine crews set their steeds loose for the climb ahead. *Colour Rail*

*Opposite:* No such drama for the crew onboard the McIntosh designed former Caledonian Railway 3F, 57568 as they potter about near their home shed with a few empty ballast wagons in between mainline trains. **Strathwood Library Collection**

*Opposite.* In the early summer of 1959, a visit to the yard at Beattock finds 72000 Clan Buchanan awaiting a path northwards with a down goods. New in December 1951, this fine locomotive would be consigned to the scrap heap in December 1962. **Colour Rail**

Thankfully the accountants and the British public would get better value out of Jubilee 45697 Achilles as it storms out of Beattock in 1960, with thirty one years service to its credit when withdrawn in September 1967. **Strathwood Library Collection**

Who could resist a stroll in the sunshine on 10 June 1962 past the engine shed 68A soon to be recoded as 66F, to take up a position north of the station at Beattock on an over-bridge to enjoy the blast off departures of northbound trains. This former Caledonian Railway engine shed would close completely on 1 May 1967. *Frank Hornby*

Both Standard Class 3MT 77005 and the waiting Black 5 have their bankers already attached for the slog northwards up the grade away from Beattock's down yard, as the Mogul gets away first. *Strathwood Library Collection*

A semi fast heads north unassisted as 72006 Clan Mackenzie arrives with a good head of steam with an up service at the point where the short branch to Moffat headed eastwards. The branch closed to passengers on 6 December 1954, and completely on 6 April, 1964. *Strathwood Library Collection*

The crew of 46226 Duchess of Norfolk have a good head of steam and they may need it as they set off past the engine shed and down yard at Beattock without a banker.
*Strathwood Library Collection*

**Branches & Byways**

*Opposite.* Stranraer shed has sent out 57340, one of Drummond's Standard Goods 2F design for the Caledonian Railway on 9 September 1961, along the one mile long stub off the Whithorn branch at Millisle, to shunt grain wagons along the dockside at Garlieston. **Strathwood Library Collection**

Right around the Scottish coastline to Banff next to join some fellow enthusiasts alongside the small engine shed by the terminus on 2 August, 1954 as the ultimately preserved Pickersgill Class D40, 62277 Gordon Highlander potters about, most likely for the benefit of the cameras. **Colour Rail**

Dropping back southwards along the North Sea coastline to Eyemouth, we see a well presented Gresley Class J39, at the station with a mixed train. Both the tide and the fishing fleet are out in the harbour in this view from June 1956. Tweedmouth shed coded 52D was home to 64813 for almost all of its existence after nationalisation, not being withdrawn until December 1962, ten months after this short branch from Burnmouth to here at Eyemouth had closed. *Colour Rail*

A small group of fellow enthuiasts match the numbers of railway staff as shunting takes place at Chirnside on 31 May 1963. Once again it would have been 52D Tweedmouth who would have sent out Ivatt Class 2MT, 46475 for this duty. The station at Chirnside was on a thirty mile long link from the ECML at Reston to St. Boswells, built by the North British Railway, passenger services through to St. Boswells having been withdrawn after major flooding of the line in 1948. But the line from Reston to Duns through Chirnside still enjoyed passengers until 1951. *Colour Rail*

Its rather rudimentary signalling and point control on the Carmylie branch that greet the crew of 62B Dundee Tay Bridge allocated 46464 on 3 September 1958. A five mile long line was constructed jointly by the Caledonian and North British Railways, under the auspices of the Dundee & Arbroath Joint Railway in 1854. Originally opened as a private railway for mineral traffic it would not be until 1900, when assent would be given under the Light Railways Act of 1896 for the carriage of passengers. This would be the first light railway to be built under the act. Very little money was invested in the four stations on the line from Elliot Junction, with the terminus here at Carmyllie being built from timber and looking very much like generous garden shed upon a platform constructed with old sleepers, just long enough to accept a single coach. The route from the junction had to climb gradients as steep as 1 in 36 with some tortuous curves in the six hundred foot climb in just the next five miles. Whilst the passengers service such as it was with just two trains each way a day, closed on 2 November 1929. However the branch remained open for goods until 24 May 1965. The line even saw the appearance of a five coach enthusiast's special on 22 April 1962 double-headed by Ivatt 2MTs 46463 and 46464 the latter we see here four years previously on a goods. *Strathwood Library Collection*

*Opposite:* Many passengers on this special headed by Standard Class 4MT 80005 have alighted for a bracing walk along the coastline at Banff Golf Club House, where there was a halt constructed three quarters of a mile from the terminus at Banff. This 2-6-4T had been sent straight to 61A Kittybrewster in November 1952 when new from Derby Works. Passenger services along this scenic branch carried on after the demise of steam in the hands of North British Bo-Bo diesels until 1964, freight continued until 1968. *Colour Rail*

Another visit to this more remote part of Scotland and the terminus at Banff in 1962 finds Standard Class 2MT 78054 setting back to run round on one of the six passenger trains each day here. Fishing was the main reason for the six mile long branch from Tillynaught being absorbed by the Great North of Scotland Railway in 1867. *John Rowe*

The sixteen mile long branch from Maud Junction to Fraserburgh was also a former Great North of Scotland Railway stronghold for their 4-4-0s in earlier years. However, by 22 June 1960 it was during the short reign of British Railways Standards on the route such as 80115 from 61A Kittybrewster here at Strichen with a modest load, this quiet station looks well kept. *Late Roy Hamilton/Strathwood Library Collection*

In contrast the former North British Railway terminus at Leslie on 19 June 1962, appears less well cared for, and why not indeed for it had been closed to passengers for thirty years at this point. Freight traffic had kept the line open, so it was included in the schedule of one of those epic Scottish rail tours this time headed appropriately by the restored former North British Railway, 256 Glen Douglas. Previously 62469 in earlier British Railways service days as a Reid designed Class D34, until withdrawn in November 1959. *Frank Hornby*

The branch is seen once again in this delightful view taken on 31 May 1966, as the train crew of a short freight headed by Gresley Class J38, 65922 attend to this gated crossing. This four and quarter mile branch from Markinch remained open to freight until 9 October, 1967. Sadly 65922 from 62A Thornton Junction didn't last that long, being withdrawn just five months after this view. *Strathwood Library Collection*

Freight traffic keeps things moving in this view on the Inverbervie branch at Gourdon in May 1959. Today its 64598 from 62B Dundee Tay Bridge in charge, this Reid 0-6-0 design for the North British Railway had been built in Glasgow during 1919, by the North British Locomotive Co. Ltd a separate entity to the railway company. The thirteen mile branch from Montrose to Inverbervie lost its passenger service on 1 October 1951. Freight as we see carried on but it too ended on 23 May 1966. As for the locomotive seen here, it was taken out of traffic in September 1962. *Colour Rail*

Freight traffic also outlasted passenger services on the branch to Whithorn, which left the mainline to Stranraer at Newton Stewart. This nineteen mile branch meandered through sleepy dairy country, with little passenger traffic one suspects even in its heyday, as wages were poor in the area. The last passenger train ran on 25 September 1950, with goods workings such as this one crossing the River Bladnoch, behind Ivatt Class 2MT 46467, taking over after the demise of the Caledonian Railway Jumbos in 1963. But this too would come to and end on 5 October 1964. *Colour Rail*

**We're All Doomed**

It was not just the branches and their stations that would be doomed as a result of the Beeching proposals. The seventy three miles of mainline from Dumfries to here at Stranraer would see closure of its passenger services in 1965, surely one of the worst cuts of the famous axe, considering the volume of road traffic bound for Stranraer and the ferries to Northern Ireland. When this scene at 67F Stranraer was recorded in June 1963, the ex Caledonian Railway Pickersgill Class 3P, 54508 had been withdrawn since the close of 1959. Whilst this former Glasgow & South Western Railway shed previously coded 68C Stranraer after nationalisation, had already lost its sub shed at Newton Stewart in February 1959. The parent shed here at Stranraer would close to steam on 27 November 1966, and completely the following February. *Rail Online*

Opposite: Another massive line closure as a result of the Beeching plans was the stretch from Carlisle to Edinburgh in 1969. The demise of the Waverley route would bring unemployment and a real loss to communities all along this ninety-eight mile route. Such as the one here at Galashiels on 30 September 1961, where we look out across the once fine flower beds to see 70018 Flying Dutchman. This Britannia had only just been recently allocated to 12C Carlisle Canal from 88A Cardiff Canton a few weeks beforehand. Notice the two young lads with the luggage trolley, being of no concern to the guard, more relaxed times indeed! *Colour Rail*

No glamour of the mainline or flower beds at Gilnockie, just a washing line on the North British Railway's branch to Langholm to greet this sole passenger on 25 May 1964. This was three weeks before closure to passengers, with freight carrying on until 18 September 1967.
*Late Roy Hamilton/Strathwood Library Collection*

*Left*. A combination of DMU and diesel locomotive arrivals, coupled with the closure of branches and goods yards across Scotland, would see large numbers of steam locomotives set aside. Such as this 1914 introduction for the Caledonian Railway, a McIntosh Class 439 0-4-4T, 55223 seen in store at Glasgow's Polmadie shed on 28 March 1959, it was withdrawn officially in September 1961. *Gerald T. Robinson*

More recent designs from the 1930s, such as these three Gresley Class V1 & V3 dumped out of use at 65C Parkhead in August 1963. The former North British shed here had been turned over to diesel in October the previous year, and closed completely two months later. Although it was still used firstly as a dump for redundant steam, then surplus diesels and for a short while preserved steam locomotives from the national collection. *Rail Photoprints*

More doomed steam locomotives at Parkhead in May 1959, with Class D11 Director, 62680 Lucy Ashton along with two classmates looking unloved awaiting what fate has in store. All but the preserved 62660 Butler Henderson from the Class D11 had long since been scrapped by the time of this view of Standard Class 5MT, 73060 being dumped out of use at Polmadie in June 1967, as modern traction and closures had seen off so many resources to the railway. *Colour Rail & Strathwood Library Collection*

*Opposite and above*. The former Great North of Scotland Railway's works at Inverurie would succumb to closure itself in 1969, however on 21 April 1962, it was very much active in scrapping the steam fleet. Such as LMS Class 2P, 40647 which had been made redundant from 67B Hurlford six months previously. Set aside alongside a failed Clayton diesel on shed at 63A Perth on 24 August 1967, was 60026 Miles Beevor, valuable souvenirs had already been removed. It was sold in February 1966 to Motherwell Machinery & Scrap, but the sale was cancelled and the engine returned to Perth on 2 August 1966. It was then taken to Crewe Works and parts were used for the restoration of 60007 Sir Nigel Gresley. It seems that the three pairs of coupled wheels on 60026 being in better condition than those of 60007 an exchange was effected. The remains of 60026 were then sold for scrap to Hughes, Bolckow of Blyth in September 1967. *Colour Rail & Jerry Beddows*

**Perth Recalled**

By the mid sixties the surviving Gresley A4s were firm favourites in Scotland on the three hour express services from Glasgow to Aberdeen, not to mention for enthusiast specials as well. These latter workings would see examples rostered all over the country, and the active fleet were kept usually in fine fettle most of the time. For 60019 Bittern, seen here in the sunshine at 63A Perth, the move away from 52A Gateshead and its reputation for filthy express locomotives in 1963 to Scotland, would be a life saver for this magnificent locomotive as it would allow time for the preservation movement to grow, and this being one of the fortunate survivors. *John Rowe*

Unfortunately no examples of the graceful Pickersgill 4-4-0s for the Caledonian Railway survived. Although this example appeared on a number of rail tours until her withdrawal from 63A Perth in October 1961, thankfully she is well recorded at least on film for the future. *Strathwood Library Collection*

*Opposite and above:* Although a generous number of Black 5s have been saved for preservation, this well presented example from Perth's one time huge fleet of these Stanier designed maids of all work sadly was not. This locomotive had been a Scottish based engine all of its life, and shows signs of being recently shopped in Glasgow with the use of their familiar larger numerals on its cabsides. Less well presented is 46244 King George VI also on shed in 1964 in its last year of traffic, based out of 12A Carlisle Kingmoor since may 1958. *Both: John Rowe*

Next on shed at Perth is an even filthier locomotive from 12A Carlisle Kingmoor, in the shape of one of their Britannias, 70009 Alfred the Great. We should perhaps still be grateful these named locomotives were still carrying their now collectable nameplates. Aside from a short stint on the Southern Region in 1951, 70009 had spent its first twelve years of service on the Eastern Region based in East Anglia, before moving to Kingmoor in late 1963. *John Rowe*

In contrast this Gresley Class V2, 60973 seen running light past the shed had spent all of its British Railways career based in this area of Scotland, with periods at both Aberdeen & Dundee as well as here at Perth in the early 1960s. The Caledonian Railway established a locomotive shed here as did The Highland Railway to service their locomotives. However it was the former Caledonian Railway's engine shed that went on to become 63A, closing to steam on 29 May 1967 and completely in October 1969. After which diesels would be stabled around the station area. *John Rowe*

Carlisle Upperby's, 46201 Princess Elizabeth finds employment on a lightly loaded express fish working on the outskirts of Perth in June 1962, perhaps it was on a Monday? Whilst the LMS built Pacific opposite was destined for preservation after being withdrawn a few months afterwards, sadly this Gresley Pacific for the LNER, seen at Perth's large station complex was not to find favour with anyone except the scrapmen. *Colour Rail & John Rowe*

Several admirers take a moment on the platforms at Perth to enjoy 60532 Blue Peter taking water whilst working The Grampian, which was the 13.30 Aberdeen - Glasgow express on 18 July 1966. This Peppercorn designed Pacific had been in much demand by enthusiasts and would see action, albeit of a troubled nature sometimes on specials as far away as the Southern Region in this its last year of British Railways service. **Bill Wright**

*Opposite.* The influence of film makers Pat Whitehouse and John Adams for their television show Railway Roundabout enabled this special pairing to double-head a normal service train from Perth to Inverness on 21 May, 1960. Regular motive power would most likely have been a single Black 5, with a pilot put on at Blair Atholl, and another perhaps at Aviemore to assist, but on this day we hark back to the reign of the 4-4-0s with this wonderful Pickersgill pairing of 54485 & 54486. **Strathwood Library Collection**

Platform end activity to be enjoyed at Perth in the steam era, meant just about everything stopping here would mean the engine crews taking water, and the driver running the back of his hand across any suspect bearings. For the road ahead would certainly mean hard work for the engine, and the fireman! On 18 July, 1966 we see home based Black 5 44998, complete with tablet catcher to assist on single line workings, running light into the station. *Bill Wright*

The next day we are greeted with not only another Class 5MT, but of the British Railways Standard variety fitted with Caprotti valve gear. This batch of St. Rollox allocated locomotives were regulars on services to and from Perth to Glasgow. They would soon give way to Sulzer powered replacements, even though these steam locomotives were barely ten years old. *Bill Wright*

One locomotive crew helps another as they change over here at Perth on 19 July 1966. This morning we have a well turned out 60034 Lord Faringdon at the head of the 08.25 Glasgow - Aberdeen. Sadly the following month would see this fine locomotive withdrawn from service. When new this A4 bore the name Peregrine after the bird of prey and was allocated the engine number 4903. The name of Lord Faringdon had previously been carried by an ex Great Central Railway, Class B3. In December 1947 this engine went for scrapping and a decision was quickly made to recognise this gentleman's continued service not only to the former Great Central Railway and to the LNER by proposing a name change to what would become 60034 under the newly nationalised railway. So it was that approval was given to make this final change of name to one of Gresley's A4s in March 1948. *Bill Wright*

The city of Perth enjoyed a large number of passenger and goods trains each day during the steam era, as a consequence both the station and the engine sheds reflected this. Travellers on this day in April 1962 would enjoy the power of Carlisle Kingmoor's 46226 Duchess of Norfolk for the journey as far as the border city as they set off with the 09.00 for Euston. A few years later and the Stanier Pacifics have been replaced, and even this array of motive power on 1 August 1965 will soon be swept away too from the city's engine shed. *Late Dave Down & Colour Rail*

*Above and opposite.* As the 1960s progressed more and more of the older types were to depart from the Perth railway scene forever, with no examples set aside for preservation. This example 54500 was withdrawn in March 1962 and 64627 from Reid's one hundred plus Class J37 by October 1963. **Mel Smith Collection & John Rowe**

Not only the more numerous locomotives, but even some of the more glamerous classes would become extinct. When this view of 72005 Clan Macgregor was taken in June 1962, we were just a few months away from the first five of her class being withdrawn en-masse that December, at a stroke of the accountants pen, five eleven-year-old locomotives written off the books. *Colour Rail*

Likewise for many of Stanier's Duchesses in this and the following year of 1963 would see the class reduced down from thirty-eight examples to twenty-two, with the last ones taken out of traffic in 1964. The Clan pictured above would work on until May 1965, whilst 46247 City of Liverpool would only make it as far as May 1963. *Colour Rail*

It was not all doom and gloom, whilst we have lost all of the Clans, although a project exists to build an eleventh one some day. Sir Billy Butlin saw the opportunity to purchase several locomotives for his holiday camps. Others went to museums both at home and in North America, and thankfully enthusiast groups and societies were formed to save not only locomotives such as 60009

Sir Nigel Gresley, seen here in the shed yard at 63A Perth during 1965. But also valuable items of rolling stock, stations, signal boxes etc and the whole that we now enjoy, fifty years after the end of regular everyday steam in Scotland. So well done to all of those both past, present and future who help preserve our rich railway heritage. *Strathwood Library Collection*

# Shed & Works Visits

*Above and opposite.* For spotters in steam days some of the more out of the way, less glamorous engine sheds were perhaps often ignored by those who were less intrepid. One such example might be 67D Ardrossan seen here from the station footbridge on 22 June 1962. Whilst surely a visit to Haymarket in Edinburgh would be high on any spotters wish list for a visit. On 8 August 1962 the new order of diesels were perhaps dominating the scene around Thompson Class A1, 60151 Midlothian. Across the city St. Margarets was still a haven for steam whilst Haymarket was officially diesel only after 8 September 1963. As for the 67D it too would lose importance becoming a sub shed to 67C Ayr in 1965 and closing completely in 1969, for a short while thereafter a dumping ground for scrap Claytons.
*Frank Hornby & Rail Online*

Fresh from a works visit in June 1963, Thompson Class B1, 61103 gets a thorough oil round before going off shed. Whilst a good number of B1s might have been seen by many a spotter, only those who ventured to the former Great North of Scotland Railway's former routes in the early 1950s would have enjoyed sights such as this Class D41, 62246 at Keith in May 1950, eking out its last few years of traffic on British Railways. *Colour Rail*

*Above and opposite.* Whilst the two diesel shunters in the background might have given good service as some are still in use today, the North British Railway, Holmes Class Y9 being repaired in the yard at 65E Kipps, on 30 April 1960, would have given sixty-four years service when withdrawn in July 1962. All enthusiasts would have wished such longevity too on this Stanier & Ivatt line up including 46257 City of Salford being attended to at Polmadie in March 1963, just nineteen months away from being withdrawn, this Pacific would be allowed just sixteen years service to British Railways.
***Colour Rail & Strathwood Library Collection***

*Above and opposite.* Contrasts with the black coal dust and oily ground at 67B Hurlford on 24 April, 1966 with the ash covered ground around the coaling shed at 65D Dawsholm on 29 April 1960. Both sheds would be swept away in 1966 and 1964 respectively in the winds of change of the 1960s. *Bill Wright & Colour Rail*

Two more contrasts with a well presented Peppercorn double chimney Class A2 60532 Blue Peter representing the class at 61B Aberdeen Ferryhill on 16 June, 1966. Compared with 60535 Hornet's Beauty at 66A Polmadie in August 1963. *Rail Photoprints & John Rowe*

*Above and opposite.* A visit to the Granite City and the former Caledonian and North British Railway's joint engine shed at Ferryhill on 17 July 1965, rewards our cameraman with this evocative view of 60006 Sir Ralph Wedgewood brewing up mightily outside the running shed. Originally as 4469 named Gadwall after a duck species, the name of the former Chief General Manager of the LNER was quickly adopted for this A4 just twelve months after it had entered service. This example of the former North British Railway Class J83 was the last one to enter service in May 1901 from Sharp Stewart & Co. Seen here at 64B Haymarket in August 1959 it would remain on the books until February 1962. **Bill Wright & Colour Rail**

The North British Railway also established another major engine shed in Edinburgh later coded as 64A St. Margarets, by the time of this view on 5 August 1965, many of the old company's locomotive types had been scrapped. Their duties either taken over by the new diesels or by more modern steam locomotives. Even the likes of 60027 Merlin was now adorned with the yellow cab stripe supposedly banning it from overhead electrified routes. Not that it would be too likely to between then and withdrawal the following February. *Colour Rail*

Thankfully no such stripe for 60024 Kingfisher the following year again at St. Margarets in September 1966. This was the month it would be withdrawn from service, I ask you, does it look like it should be sent for scrap? Especially in front of the Clayton standing in shame behind it on the other side of the ashpits! *Strathwood Library Collection*

*Above and opposite.* Resplendent and returned to its post war livery and number in preservation, the former 60007 Sir Nigel Gresley shows off in the sunshine at 66A Polmadie in 1967, as another Type 1 Clayton, lurks in the background. Carlisle enjoyed three engine sheds during the British Railways steam era, the former LNWR shed at Kingmoor, the often forgotten ex Midland Railway shed at Durran Hill which closed in 1959, and the former North British Railway established their foothold in the city here at Canal. Coded 68A, until 1 February 1958, when it became 12B as part of the London Midland Region. On this day 60068 Sir Visto is dressed to head The Waverley, a named express from St. Pancras to Edinburgh Waverley.

**Strathwood Library Collection & Colour Rail**

*Left and below.* We couldn't resist another superb view of 60024 Kingfisher during September 1966 on shed at 64A St. Margarets. This angle shows the ashpit and the descent for removing this by-product of the steam locomotive well. No such arrangement at 65D Dawsholm on 29 April 1960, as Class J35/5 64471 is being disposed. The empty wagons in the background this time on the incline upwards are from feeding the coaling plant. *Colour Rail*

*Opposite and above.* The program of fitting double chimneys to Class A3s began in 1958 and ended in 1960. Built in 1929 at Doncaster Works, 60096 *Papyrus* seen here on shed at 62B Dundee Tay Bridge was named after the winner of the 1923 Derby at Epsom. Dalry Road shed was coded 64C, and established by the Caledonian Railway on the line into Edinburgh Princes Street. Time was running out for both 57634 and for the shed here in 1962, as the locomotive went for scrap the following year, and both Dalry Road shed and Princes Street station closed in 1965.

**Colour Rail & Robin Brown Collection**

*Above and opposite:* A change of direction for both 60034 Lord Faringdon and the locomotives to be found on shed, here at 61B Aberdeen Ferryhill in 1965. Another visit on 17 July that year finds a number of diesels beginning to appear in this part of north east Scotland. Steam would be officially ousted from the shed on 18 March 1967. In 1950, there was an allocation of forty steam locomotives here and a further seventy across the Granite City at 61A Kittybrewster. *John Rowe & Bill Wright*

*Above and opposite:* In both the Caledonian Railway and LMS days this location was known as Balornock, the shed replaced cramped affairs both within St. Rollox Works and at Buchanan Street. In British Bailways days it became known as St. Rollox, we see Standard 4MT 76102 here in August 1965, and a recently ex-shops Austerity, 90386 in October 1964. ***Strathwood Library Collection***

From a Caley fortress, to the North British stronghold at 64B Haymarket to enjoy Class D34, 62492 Glen Garvin being turned in 1956. *Colour Rail*

Nestled along the banks of the Union Canal, 64E Polmont is home to Class J36 65311 Haig on 22 April, 1962.
*Colour Rail*

At 64F Bathgate on 29 May, 1964 the scraplines in the background look plentiful as Class J37, potters up the shed yard. *Rail Photoprints*

Opposite: The thoroughbred Gresley lines of 60057 Ormonde may well be clean but she has been doctored with smoke deflectors here at 64B Haymarket by October 1961. *Colour Rail*

*Above and opposite:* There are two differing designs of water crane in the shed yard at 62A Thornton Junction alongside Class J37, 64625 stabled next to the coaling plant on 16 July, 1965. The building in the background houses within it the winding towers of the then modern Rothes Colliery. Close by in the shed yard the same day, Standard Class 5MT, 73010 has worked its way north from 9H, Patricroft in Manchester. **Both: Bill Wright**

The former Caledonian Railway's engine shed at Motherwell, coded 66B was a must for many wanting to catch a last sight of Riddles 2-10-0s, especially as they were being withdrawn during 1961 and 1962. Examples lay dumped also at Kingmoor, Grangemouth and Carstairs. *Strathwood Library Collection*

*Opposite:* A mixed condition trio of Standard Class 4MTs are being shunted about the shed yard at 67A Corkerhill on 9 April, 1964 by soon to be withdrawn 80021 on its home shed. *Colour Rail*

The former Glasgow & South Western Railway's engine shed at Hurlford, coded 67B in British Railways days appears to offer the visitor little except this ex Caledonian Class 3F, 56368 in April 1961. *Strathwood Library Collection*

*Above and opposite*. A return to 62A Thornton Junction on 26 August 1966 in a search for the now diminishing steam fleet working the Fife coal field, yields Austerity, 90441 on its home shed, just weeks away from being withdrawn. Far cleaner and much more colourful are the preserved Highland Railway's Jones Goods, 103 and the Great North of Scotland Railway's Class D40, 49 Gordon Highlander as a backdrop to Class 3F 57581 being turned at Aberdeen Ferryhill as part of a railtour on 17 June 1962. *Both: Colour Rail*

# Highland Flings

*Above and opposite.* In the middle of one of those epic five day rail tours around the Scottish Region on 15 June, 1960, this one was arranged by both the Stephenson Locomotive Society and the RCTS. On this morning at Inverness we have the preserved Highland Railway Jones Goods, 103 making ready for the departure south along the old company's new mainline to Perth. Two years later and it's the Caledonian Railway's 123 and the North British Railway's 256 Glen Douglas drawing the crowds at Oban on 12 May 1962, this colourful pairing will head for Glasgow Buchanan Street, via the Callander route. *Frank Hornby & Mike Morant Collection*

*Left:* In the mid 1950s the growth of car ownership was yet to happen and if you wanted to get anywhere in the highlands, the railway was perhaps your best choice. A lengthy double-headed southbound train makes a stop for passengers at this crossing point, whilst a Class K2 has a single coach within a goods train bound for Fort William. The cameraman is standing on the main A82 trunk road to capture the steep slopes of Ben Vorlich in the background. **Colour Rail**

*Opposite:* Passengers queue for the Macbraynes ferry service across Loch Eil from the station forecourt at the old Fort William station in August 1959, although the sun is shining, one suspects there is both a chill and a shower in the air from their attire. Meanwhile one of Gresley's Class K2/2s, 61782 Loch Quoich, looks like she has been worked hard by her driver. **Colour Rail**

*Above and opposite.* Such was the draw of these epic enthusiast railtours, the one arranged for 1962 lasted for nine days. Starting from Perth on 14 June and ending at Carlisle on 23 June, having travelled across just about every possible route available to the tour within the Scottish Region. This is Black 5, 44978 on the second day heading from Inverness to Georgemas Junction, where the Jones Goods was waiting. Here it is crossing the Kyle of Sutherland at Invershin, with Carbisdale Castle in the background. Plenty of time at Garelochead in July 1959, for the relaxed crew to refresh the tanks of one of the last two surviving Reid Class C15s, 67474 both this example and 67460, were based at 65A Eastfield. **Colour Rail & Strathwood Library Collection**

*Above and opposite:* The other surviving Class C15, 67460 is seen here making a spirited departure from Arrochar towards Craigendoran on 19 September 1959. They would both be withdrawn the following April, just before the summer timetable was released. would be withdrawn in April, 1960 leaving 67474 seen overleaf to soldier on. The DMU coach in the background here at the usually tranquil Killin Junction on 25 July 1964, has most likely been put off with a hot box, and awaits collection. Meanwhile we can enjoy Standard Class 4MT, 80093 running around its single coach for the branch down to Killin.

**David Cobbe Collection/Rail Photoprints & Colour Rail**

Down at the truncated terminus at Killin in August 1965 we can see how the highland weather has taken its toll on the wooden station building. On this day it's the turn of Standard 4MT, 80028 from 63A Perth to run the service back along the highly scenic five mile branch to Killin Junction. *Strathwood Library Collection*

The Standard Class 4MTs took over from the Caledonian Railway's 0-4-4Ts, and on another visit to Killin in 1964 we can see the manoeuvre to gravity shunt and run round as 80092 this time has charge. The branch and the mainline via Callander were hit listed by Dr. Beeching anyway, but the landslip at Glenogle on the main line, brought about closure here on 28 September, 1965. *Strathwood Library Collection*

*Opposite:* On 13 April 1963, its 80092 on duty again on the branch back up at Killin Junction as a snow storm greets the Caledonian Single and the tour participants on their arrival. *Rail Photoprints*

To enjoy the highland scenery the Scottish Region put two observation cars into good use, this one once from the Southern Railway's Devon Belle service, and is seen here at Kyle of Lochalsh in 1960 on a working with 49 Gordon Highlander, and again from the passengers viewpoint near Helensburgh. The other was the former LNER beavertail SC1719E seen at Fort William on 2 June 1963.
**Strathwood Library Collection & Colour Rail**

*Above and opposite.* The North British carved their route to pick up the once lucrative fish traffic from the west coast here at Mallaig. On this day we find Peppercorn Class K1, 62012 from 63A Fort William on duty in 1962. It was the whisky traffic that would be the lifeblood of the lines through Speyside on the former Great North of Scotland Railways route, as here at Auchendachy with Class D40 62262, on 2 August, 1954. This graceful 4-4-0 would be sent for scrap in October the following year and amazingly the station would not close until 1968. **Robin Brown Collection & Colour Rail**

*Opposite and this page:* We catch 62262 with that same working once again in the beautiful countryside of Speyside. These Pickersgill locomotives were progressively withdrawn during the early 1950s leaving 62277 Gordon Highlander, seen here at Elgin as the sole survivor to be preserved after 1958. In sight of the River Spey at Craigellachie, we see 62271 and then another 62274 Benachie by the turntable at the small shed here in April, 1954. ***All: Colour Rail***

Two Black 5s cross on passenger workings at Grantown-on-Spey West on 10 September, 1959. This station was situated on the former Highland Railway's original mainline from Perth to Inverness via Dava. Members of the Strathspey Railway hope to bring the railway back here one day, and to rebuild a station here as their northern terminus of their route along the scenic River Spey at this point. Meanwhile their base for maintenance of their rolling stock is here at Aviemore, where we see a view looking out from the shed in April 1961. On this day Fairburn Class 4MT, 42168 in residence at its then home shed coded 60B.
***Colour Rail & Strathwood Library Collection***

*Opposite.* Unfortunately the memorable water tower at 60A Inverness was demolished along with the open roundhouse when the shed here was due be closed to steam in February 1962. The presence of BRCW built Type 2 diesels suggests the days for Black 5, 45117 being welcome here might be drawing to a close, it would be sent away formally in April, 1962. ***Colour Rail***

*Above and opposite.* Blast off from Inverness just above sea level southwards in July, 1957 for this double-headed pairing of Black 5s. In the next twenty-three miles they will have to climb 1,315 feet to the first summit at Slochd.

Another duo of Black 5s ease into Killiecrankie's once spacious platforms in the early 1960s, sadly the station would close in 1965.
*Colour Rail & Robin Brown Collection*

Another pair of Black 5s, are caught at Gleneagles around 1960 on passenger duties. This was the junction station for the Crieff branch, which would close firstly to passengers on 6 July, 1964 and then a few months later to goods on 2 November. *Robin Brown Collection*

Built by the LMS at Derby in October, 1929 to a design by Fowler, clearly influenced by similar designs for the Midland Railway. Perhaps 40614 has seen some care and attention with a paintbrush recently, as it will soon depart Dumfries for Kilmarnock on a sunny day in 1959.
*David Cobbe Collection/Rail Photoprints*

*Above and opposite.* The wires had been erected for the Blue Trains at Glasgow Central which went live in 1962, but the Caledonian Railway opened their magnificent station originally in 1879. On 1 August 1966, steam activity was getting a bit thin here so the sight of Standard Class 4MT, 76004 was worthy of a shot by our cameraman. The rival Glasgow & South Western Railway established their terminus at St. Enoch in 1876. It too was an elegant affair as can be seen above Jubilee 45740 Munster, unfortunately it was decreed it should be dispensed with and closed in 1966.

**Michael Beaton & Colour Rail**

Two views from 1965, firstly at Glasgow Buchanan Street on Monday 7 June 1965, as the crew of this Caprotti valve gear fitted Standard Class 5MT, 73152 await departure. This was the Caledonian Railway's original terminus for the city opened in 1849, it would be also be closed in 1966. Whilst the junction station here at Newton Stewart was another victim of the infamous axe, as Standard 4MT, 80061's train seems well patronised just before closure in 1965. *Peter Coton & Colour Rail*

*Above and opposite:* We have already touched on how the closures from the Beeching Plan have effected communities, considering just how much traffic was generated through the Port of Stranraer it must have made more sense to retain the line back through Newton Stewart towards Dumfries and on to Carlisle. In 1964, Black 5, 45120 from Carlisle Kingmoor will head down this soon to be closed route with a stopper in between sailings to Northern Ireland, whilst the DMU on the right will head for Ayr. In 1962, its Black 5, 45477 that has possession of the line along with the engineers at Mid Calder. **Strathwood Library Collection & Robin Brown**

Opposite: Down by the lineside once more, this time at South Queensferry in 1963 with the construction of the then new road crossing well advanced in the background. However for this Holmes Class J36, 65288 its seventy years of service are approaching retirement, which will come four years later as one of the last three of her class in service. **Robin Brown Collection**

The wisdom behind the construction of Standard Class 2MT, 78049 at Darlington in late 1955 as the Modernisation Plan was being published, beggars belief. As the bureaucrats would render this state investment redundant eleven years later, in their head long rush to modernise the railway. But all seemed peaceful at Tweedmouth on 15 August, 1961 six weeks into the tenure of Dr. Beeching as the Chairman of the British Railways Board. **Colour Rail**

Mixed traffic Class 5MT power at Stirling, firstly with the Robin Riddles designed Standard Caprotti 5MT, 73149. When seen on 18 August, 1966 it was working an early evening service from Buchanan Street to Dunblane. Sent new from Derby Works in March 1957 to 65B St. Rollox, its first and only re-allocation would occur a few weeks after this shot was taken, when in October it was sent here to 65J Stirling. Not a good move, as it was then withdrawn soon after in December. Whilst, 44921 was just one of 63A Perth's multitude of Black 5s when it was seen running light past the shed at Stirling in 1964, a year before it too was declared surplus and withdrawn.
*Strathwood Library Collection*

It's the school holidays in early August 1964, and a number of local lads are on hand at Carstairs to watch Fairburn Class 4MT, 42056 couple up to a lame Black 5. *Colour Rail*

Its almost departure time at Kilmarnock in July 1960 for Fowler Class 2P 40661 in more ways than one as the works here was already busy cutting up a number of her classmates, this example would go for scrap in 1961. *Colour Rail*

After World War Two, 4-4-0 designs were viewed by management as old fashioned and every opportunity was taken to replace them with six coupled designs. Among these out of favour classes were the Gresley Class D49s, this is 62744 The Holderness at Thornton Junction in 1957. Seventy-six had been handed to British Railways in 1948, indeed sixty-six were still in traffic when this photograph was taken, However, by the end of 1959 they were down to just twenty-two examples and by the close of 1961 they were all gone, save for 67212 Morayshire, which thankfully was saved for preservation.

*Strathwood Library Collection*

Meanwhile during the period of British Railway's construction of new steam locomotives, including the designs from the pre-nationalisation companies, five hundred and seventy seven, 4-6-0s were built. Included within this total was Black 5, 44674 which was built at Horwich and went into service during March, 1950. We see it running light engine through Larbert on 28 August, 1965. *Strathwood Library Collection*

During this same period nine hundred and ninety tank locomotives, to various designs were built for the nationalised railway, of which seven hundred and sixty would be to designs from the era of the big four companies. Among the exceptions would be one hundred and fifty five of these Standard Class 4MT tanks, such as 80006 still at work as a pilot for Edinburgh Waverley among the diesel invasion on 21 June, 1963. *Strathwood Library Collection*

During the era of steam perhaps the workaday 0-6-0 designs may have lacked the glamour or attractions of other types, but they formed the backbone of much of the shorter distance freight workings. Among their numbers were the Gresley Class J38, such as 65934 here approaching Thornton Junction in 1965, on this day sent out with the depot's steam crane. The entire class of thirty five engines spent most of their days working the Fife coalfield. *Strathwood Library Collection*

Among these truly Scottish 0-6-0s were the one hundred and four Reid designed Class J37 for the former North British Railway. These would be the most powerful 0-6-0s built for a Scottish railway. This is 64620 working a local trip freight at Dundee in July, 1966. They also put in some sterling work on passenger duties too. *Rail Photoprints*

Whereas tender first running with an 0-6-0 design could be most unpleasant for so many reasons. Engine crews must have found the likes of Standard Class 4MT, 80123 a much more desirable proposition, for work where timings or facilities precluded the chance of turning. This is the 66A Polmadie, allocated engine making smoke at Port Glasgow on 6 July, 1965.
*John A. M. Vaughan/Rail Photoprints*

Its hard work and toil for 67C Ayr's 42800, as the locomotive crew give the Crab a good go on a rake of empties at Holehouse Junction in 1963. *Colour Rail*

Everything on 7 May, 1960 should be a lot easier for the crew of Pickersgill Class 3P, 54465 as they have an enthusiast's tour for the day, taking a stop at Cathcart here as the wires are up for the Blue Trains already. *Strathwood Library Collection*

**Specials**

This page and opposite. It was a treat for all concerned to see the four restored Scottish pre-grouping locomotives at work in the late 1950s and early 1960s. On 19 April, 1965, 123 & 49 Gordon Highlander create a stir at Carstairs. Whilst the Jones Goods recalls times gone by at Dalwhinnie as the 4-6-0 slakes its thirst on 15 June, 1960.
*Strathwood Library Collection & Frank Hornby*

*Opposite:* That same headboard adorns 256 Glen Douglas at Alloa, a few days later on 17 June 1960 during that great tour proudly boasting its coverage of lines and locomotives of the four constituent Scottish railway companies. The preserved Class D34 would be the only engine for the tour on this the last of the five days. Starting from Perth and shuffling all around at least eight counties, before setting off its no doubt weary, but satisfied participants at Glasgow Central, to make their own way homewards thereafter.
**Strathwood Library Collection**

By the autumn of 1963, the writing was on the wall for Stanier's flagship class of Duchesses. Prompted by class withdrawals the RCTS arranged a special from Crewe to here at Edinburgh Princes Street and return on 5 October, 1963. Crewe supplied 46251 City of Nottingham as the motive power throughout, this locomotive would make a further three appearances the following year on various rail tours around the regions, before its demise in September 1964.

It was not just prestige types that were in demand for specials as they were fast disappearing, this duo of Class J37s 64570 & 64618 at Edinburgh Waverley on 25 June, 1965. *Strathwood Library Collection*

Tour participants are not deterred by a drop of rain on 5 June 1965 at Edinburgh Waverley for what might be their last chance for a run behind 60052 Prince Palatine. *Strathwood Library Collection*

As a special, the RCTS & SLS Joint Scottish Tour between 14 - 23 June, 1962 used twenty-one different locomotives, this is Fairburn Class 4MT, 42277 from 66A Polmadie at Catrine, this location has lost its passengers services in 1943. *Frank Hornby*

*This page and opposite.* Among the selection of locomotives provided for this marathon tour was Black 5, 44978 which 60A Inverness shed supplied for a number of legs on four days of the tour. This is on day three, where it will be the motive power for a run to Aviemore via the original Highland Railway's route across Dava Moor. The next day it would be the turn of McIntosh Class 812, 57581 from 66A Polmadie to do the honours for most of the day, including this trip to Brechin. *Strathwood Library Collection*

In comparison the four day tour of the SLS as their Scottish Rambler No.2 over Easter 1963, was a more lightweight affair perhaps, with fourteen locomotives being used. Here we are on the last day as Jubilee 45588 Kashmir, has been stopped to await clearance of the single line ahead along the Port Road from Dumfries to Stranraer, at Loch Skerrow near Gatehouse of Fleet. A chance for everyone to stretch their legs and enjoy the wild Galloway countryside for themselves. *Richard Icke*

We have already mentioned in the photographer's introduction we see 60027 Merlin at Riccarton Junction after it was put on at Carlisle to replace the failed 60052 Prince Palatine we saw on page 141. The A4 took the tour back to Edinburgh Waverley on Saturday 5 June, 1965. The badge affixed to the boiler sides is for HMS Merlin, the Royal Naval Air Station at Donibristle in Fife, they were awarded to the locomotive in May 1946. *Peter **Coton***

*Both pages:* Flying the flag for the west coast Anglo - Scottish route we see 46201 Princess Elizabeth from 66A Polmadie, providing a majestic sight at Glasgow Central in 1959. Whereas 64B Haymarket have provided this filthy Class A2, 60529 Pearl Diver for traffic on this day in 1961 at Edinburgh Waverley on the east coast route, hardly a shining example. **Colour Rail & Robin Brown Collection**

*Both pages:* To observe religious sensitivities on a Sunday the headboard has been reversed on this day for 60025 Falcon, as the crew observe the permanent way occupation here at Burnmouth in August, 1960. No such observance of reversed headboards in this view at Carlisle in 1956, as Royal Scot, 46140 The King's Royal Rifle Corps. and 46222 Queen Mary swap over on The Royal Scot. **Colour Rail & Dave Cobbe Collection/Rail Photoprints**

*Both pages:* The platform ends at Perth were a popular spot to record the graceful lines of Gresley's Class A4s, although on this day in 1965 the condition of 60007 Sir Nigel Gresley would be of concern to the great man.

For at least two of the young spotters of the day at Glasgow Central in the mid 1950s, the sights and sounds of 72000 Clan Buchanan departing hardly warrant a second glance. *John Rowe & Colour Rail*

The boiler casing of Peppercorn Class A2, 60528 Tudor Minstrel looks well burnished by the cleaners when this unknown cameraman recorded it making a brief stop for passengers at Larbert in May, 1966 just a few months short from the end of its eighteen year career on British Railways ending as a 61B Aberdeen Ferryhill locomotive. **Strathwood Library Collection**

Another Doncaster built product was Thompson Class A1, 60152 Holyrood taking water on a cold morning at St. Boswells on the Waverley Route during January, 1962. For this 64B Haymarket engine, a service career of just sixteen years would be managed when withdrawn from 50A York in June, 1965. *Dave Cobbe Collection/Rail Photoprints*

*Both pages*. Two platform end views at Buchanan Street station in Glasgow during steam's final flings on the three hour Aberdeen expresses. Firstly 60024 Kingfisher makes a fine sight as her crew await the signal to back out for servicing in May, 1966. On 21 July, 1966 it was the turn of 60532 Blue Peter on a similar working as they have just received the peg to move off. *Colour Rail & Dave Hill*

Take your pick between a red Duchess on a rake of maroon coaches such as 46247 City of Liverpool on a down service at Carstairs in 1960, against green liveried 46249 City of Sheffield going well at Lamington the following year. Both of these fine locomotives would be withdrawn during 1963 to the disappointment of hundreds of enthusiasts and railwaymen alike. *Colour Rail*

# Also of interest from Strathwood to collect

London Midland Steam Days Remembered
London Midland Steam Days Remembered II
Eastern Steam Days Remembered

Sixties Spotting Days around the Scottish Region

Seventies Spotting Days around the Scottish Region

Looking back at English Electric Locomotives
Looking back at Deltics
Looking back at Class 50 Locomotives
Looking back at Class 37 Locomotives
Looking back at Class 26 & 27 Locomotives
Looking back at Class 47 Locomotives

SYPHON SALUTE 50 Years of Class 37s

Glasgow Central, Central to Glasgow
Scottish Railways Two Decades in Transition

Published by Strathwood, 9 Boswell Crescent,
Inverness, IV2 3ET. Tel 01463 234004
www.strathwood.co.uk

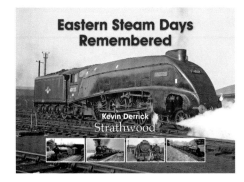

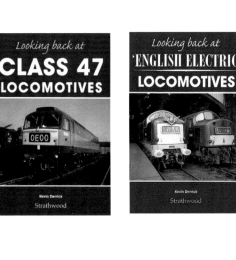